Life's a Beach

Life's a Beach
SPF 15

Don't Get Burned Out

Maggie Brumit

ACKNOWLEDGEMENTS

To all who are going through something and need support, guidance, a reality check, or just something to read to take you away from where you are, I dedicate this book to you.

Thank You, God
for the path to understanding and peace within

To Danny, Chelsea, Andy, and Kayleigh
my best friends, my loving family and support system

To My Sisters, Karen, Patricia and Charlotte
my life coaches

To My Brothers Harold and David
for the school of hard knocks

To My Mom, Dad, and Tom
forever in our hearts

**Last but Most Definitely Not Least,
To My Dear Friend Teresa**
for your never ending encouragement and support

Contents

PREFACE

A re you at the end of the rope, your rope? Is your world spinning faster than 24/7? Do you need to find peace in your journey?

I am here to help. I wrote this to inspire those of you going through trials in your life; whether it is financial, marriage, children, sickness, death, or what you would consider an issue in your life. Not all situations can be rated the same, even though a lot of the components making up the issues are the same. We are all different; we are unique. One way of handling issues may not be perfect for everyone.

My years on this earth has been going from one struggle to another. Growing up, our family did not have much by way of stuff. My mother and father conceived and raised 7 children together. There was 14 years difference between the first born and last (myself). We were a family of 9 and our father provided the best he could for us. We went through health, financial, and social struggles. I once thought that we were so poor we had to be the only family that ate as many potatoes as we did. Dad would go to a vegetable stand called "Potato Town" weekly to buy a fifty-pound bag of potatoes. If we had anything, it was a potato - fried potatoes, mashed potatoes, stewed potatoes and the list goes on. My brothers and sisters had to help out a lot to make the family function and help get through the daily chores. There were times we did not know what tomorrow would bring but we always found a way to make do with what we had. We had each other and in that, what we had was everything.

At 18, I left the nest called home and went on to marry the love of my life. That is how it is supposed to be, right? Live happily ever after and always. No! Life's struggles did not end when my new life began.

I was 18, my boyfriend and I went away for the weekend and he proposed to me in the mountains of Skyline Drive Virginia. It was perfect at the time but time did change. We lost 2 children to miscarriage and through much planning and trial, we did eventually have a beautiful baby girl. We bought a home and then got married four years into our relationship. Not the storybook life, or the one to be considered acceptable by some as a start to life, but it was the path we traveled and that was perfect for us. When our daughter was four, she began to break bones easily without bruising or swelling.

Preface

We went through many years in and out of the doctor offices, hospitals, and emergency rooms with her. It did not end there. In the midst of this, my brother was diagnosed with cancer. I was trying to tend to my daughter's needs, enjoy what would be the last 6 months of my brother's life and work a full-time job in a busy office at the same time.

I would take my brother to church on Sundays with my daughter and myself. It was a small hometown church. I would have to help him into the wheelchair and get him to the car. It wasn't as easy as it sounds, though, the ramp from my father's home was not your average handicap ramp. It was more like an Evel Knievel stunt ramp. One day, I beat the wheelchair to the car after I fell under it and slid all way down. It doesn't sound fun, but he and I were ok and we had many laughs over it. We also went for Sunday drives and stopped by the local town park to eat lunch and talk frequently. That was nice but short lived. My brother was going for chemo treatments, but his blood counts dropped and he had to have a blood transfusion. He seemed like a new man after that but that was short lived as well. The doctors told us we had two weeks left with him at most. The very next day, when I arrived to visit with him, my father told me that the doctor said we had two days left now! Two days! That was

3

not fair. I had already been feeling cheated with time when I thought I had two weeks. I was getting pressure from my job along with the stress of wanting to be there for his every last breath. My brother passed from metastatic cancer in less than a day after being told he had two days. We made his funeral arrangements. My father kept it together when we were around, but my mother told me he cried like a baby at night about the loss of my brother. I felt so sad for my father while I too was grieving over my brother. It was a rough year with his passing. My daughter continued to have many visits to the doctor for her health issues and I became pregnant and delivered our son in the same year.

It was a year after my brother had passed that my mother took ill. She was diagnosed with pancreatic cancer. We were going back and forth to Johns Hopkins to visit doctors for her care. All of this happening while I continued to work the full-time demanding job, caring for my daughter's health needs, and tending to my household duties. We went through many visits to the doctor in Baltimore and it was decided that my Mother would have the "Whipple Procedure" to remove her pancreatic tumor. Her survival from this procedure depended on many variables, one being whether the tumor was attached to the main artery. Well, it was attached, which was not good news. In the end, it was a very short time frame from my Mother being diagnosed with pancreatic cancer to having the Whipple procedure and to passing, all within three months.

I didn't know the next day would be the last time I could ever speak to her again. It all hit me as I lay on the bed next to my mom the night before she passed. Life is short, people come and go, we come and we leave this world alone. I knew I was going to be missing her soon, but you really never know when soon will come. I have to say, that night I spent with her gave me the best hour of my life obtaining answers to questions I didn't even know I had, experiencing her deep knowledge and endless wit. Getting to know the person I thought I knew wholly but little did I know; 25 years was not enough to know much really as time would tell and the years would pass without her.

Losing my mother was extremely hard on me but more so for our father who had been married to the love of his life, my mother, for a few months shy of 42 years when she passed. He was heartbroken and lonely. My father would stay weekends with me and I tried my best to take his mind off of mom's passing.

You could see my mother in his eyes as he would reminisce about her, and the ache it left in his heart could be felt in his blank stare. This heartache is the reason I believe his health quickly declined. He was not the easiest to persuade to visit a doctor. This was a stressful time as I was grieving on the inside trying to be strong for him and my family on the outside.

About three years after my Mom passed away, I had to have hernia surgery. A few days out of surgery, I told my father I would come visit him, but I did not feel well, so I called him to let him know I could not be there. He seemed ok on the phone. It was the next day that my father had a massive stroke, leaving him bedridden unable to speak or feed himself. That devastated me with guilt and pain. The whys' and what ifs' flooded my mind. If only I had visited when I said I would, could I have prevented this from happening to him? I had to quickly put those emotions aside as I had been in charge of his care at that time. I had to learn at a moments notice how to be a home caregiver in a way I have never been trained. I had to give him insulin shots, feed him, and crush pills to give through the feeding tube, change his adult diapers, bath him in the bed, know when and how to roll him and pull him up into bed safely to avoid bed sores, and use a lift to put him in a reclining chair. I managed to do this with 2 small children to care for and continue to work. At this period in my life, I was able to bring work home, but my co-workers did not agree with my absence at the office so that was definitely not going to work. Our family was very distraught. My brothers, sisters, and I worked out a plan of home care so my father would not have to be in a nursing home. At the time, I devoted 2 nights and a weekend day to assist with the care of my father; my sister gave up her job to be with him during the weekdays and my brother cared for him through the night and the evenings I was not there. This was not easy. My daughter always seemed to break a bone or need to go to the emergency room on my night to care for my father. This made tensions build between my brother and me.

I continued to assist with the care of my father, care for my children and their health needs, but now not only was I working full-time, I was also working part-time and taking college courses. I was not sure if I was coming or going some days. On top of it all, my daughter was diagnosed with "RSD" Reflex Sympathetic Dystrophy. Chronic pain disease that was brought on by a traumatic fall down our home stairs that left her temporarily paralyzed for 3 days. This led to many more hospital stays as her skin would burn as if she were on fire, not being able to walk or tolerate clothing on her skin. When she broke a bone, and she definitely did that many times, they would have to cast her leg but cut the cast off and add Velcro to make the cast removable. Her skin would turn purple and red under the cast so we would have to remove it frequently. She had to be enrolled in online homeschool for the remainder of her high school career due to her many hospital visits and unpredictable health issues. She was not allowed to go to her high school senior prom due to being what was considered home schooled. This really made her feel heartbroken at the time. I truly believe that dealing with so much and staying strong for so long finally led to my decline in health. I developed Lupus, causing much fatigue and joint pain. It also caused brain fog and that is when my sister and I decided it would be best if I stopped caring for my father to tend to my health needs. They so graciously took over the task, which lasted another eight years until my father passed. He suffered so much in silence, but he had the best care to get him through.

My husband became ill with COPD, Diabetes and a page full of ailments that caused him to become disabled. He required and continues to require many doctor visits and much care as he has more bad than good days with his health. In my son's junior year of high school, he became ill and was put on homeschool. We had many

8

doctor visits and testing to find out what he was dealing with. We worked out a physical therapy program and medication to get him back on his feet. That was the shortest (about six months) anyone has had a health issue in my family.

This overview is just a lens into my life, a brief glimpse into what I have been through in my years on this earth and continue to go through. Although it has not been easy, my experiences have taught me to seek peace and strength. I always find ways to laugh at everything because life is very short.

The point I want to convey to you is about perception - the way you think about or understand someone or something. How we define ourselves can often come from our perception and how we are trained or how we believe that makes this perception a reality to us. That is deep! And as you read further, you will see how deep and controlling our perceptions can be. I hope you find my inspirations helpful in your own unique way. I am passing along information that has helped many people manage stress, their perceptions, and how to deal with them. (It will help you stress in a good way).

You will notice I did not use chapters in this book. Chapters are what we go through in life. I call them inspirations because it is the inspiration that leads us through the chapters of our lives, the lessons that teach. Life is short, the walk may not be a stroll on the beach but Life's a Beach if you learn to enjoy and stay true to yourself no matter what situation you are in or what path you take.

INSPIRATION 1 – LIFE

Have You Arrived At Wit's end? At times you feel like curling up into a ball and rolling away. You don't see a light at the end of the tunnel, a dark hole has now become your life. Give yourself some self-pity time; it's yours, you've earned it!

I like to call it my "SPF 15". It sounds more relaxing and that is already a head start on the issue at hand. Self-Pity Factor 15, a time to gripe, groan, and/or let yourself feel sorry about your situation. Be mad, be sad, be happy, be whatever it is that will allow you the time to feel the emotions you have been led to by the situation at hand. Although I can't judge how much time that is for each person's situation, I will advise you to give it to yourself but do not over indulge. Like anything else in life, over indulging is not going to fix the problem.

It was a long road that led me to understand this and I want to help you deal with all the bumps and turns I had to travel to get to a life of peace among the chaos.

RAINBOW OF LIFE

(Colors of many faces)

If looks could kill, you would be locked up by now! You know you have done it, admit it - someone totally gets on your last nerve and just plays it like a violin. You are boiling inside, busting at the seams. You hold it in because you have to or else...

Or else what? You will look like a fool overreacting to a situation. Maybe the other person (you know the one peeving you off) has one of those personalities that always make them look like a victim even when they are really a little devil inside. They may be the type of person that knows how to play people, especially those of higher authority than you. (These are the kind of people that make you look like you are about to have or are going through a nervous breakdown). Or you are one of those people that when you go off the handle (or flip your lid as I like to call it), people think you have lost it and are over reacting because you never do that. They look at you as if you have three heads and turn the tides to make it seem like you are whacked out, losing it, and out of control.

Maybe you have been dealt a trying journey in life. A person you loved dearly has passed away. You feel as if you have not done anything to deserve the cards you have been dealt and life is taking it out on you, bending you in so many ways you just feel you could snap. Maybe this seems to happen to you all the time and you cannot seem to get a break. You're constantly feeling like

> ### *Maggieism*
> Some people will try to make you feel small but continue to see big and you will overcome.
> ~Maggie Brumit

something is keeping you from your destiny and holding you down.

Your life seems to have constant sorrow and grief. People are always on the opposite side of where you are and you can't find a paddle to row. You have hit a brick wall and there is no place to go or be. It is a cold, dark place. The sun doesn't shine. You are almost emotionally comatose and have succumbed to the situation or issue. It overshadows everything in your life and you cannot see past it. You walk around almost zombified just mottling through the have to's of the daily grind.

Some of you may contemplate why you should stay here and think of suicide, running away, or even harm others. Although you haven't done so, it may have crossed your mind. I have been to this lonely deserted island and I have contemplated many not so nice things. It hurts, a very low place where life doesn't seem enjoyable and even something as simple as a child's laugh doesn't bring a smile to your face or inner soul anymore. I have been there, so let me help you. It really is not as bad as it seems no matter the situation. Walk with me and let's take a journey to redeem your mind, body, and soul. Be a victor not a victim of any circumstance.

Come back to me, I have put you in a very sad place, purposely. This is the time to step back, take a look at the situation. Take your SPF 15! This would be a prime time to re-evaluate your mind, body, and soul connection to better grasp the situation. Don't forget to look at yourself inside and out as sometimes we overlook ourselves in the mirror. It can be hard to accept that we may need to change ourselves to move forward with this person, issue, or trying times. Even after you have looked in the mirror to accept any changes needed on your part, there are some you cannot move forward with, no matter how hard you try, so don't be too hard on yourself.

> *Maggieism*
> Remember this,
> People only make
> you feel how you
> let them make
> you feel.
> ~Maggie Brumit

This process can be very trying. Consider it just like shampoo, you may have to reapply and repeat the steps along the way! Remember, just breathe. Today may be a fiery pit of over boiling PU Stew, but tomorrow is a new day. I know it's easier said than done, I understand this as well. Stay strong, my friend, stay strong.

INSPIRATION 2 – STRENGTH

(Stay Strong Survival Guide)

How do you stay strong? This is a tough question. What does strong mean? It doesn't have to be like the going to the gym lifting weights type of strong. Inner strength is built by your way of handling situations and emotions. It's about building an inner core of mind, body, and soul connection to keep you going in any situation.

This is not as easy as it sounds. Some people say, "What doesn't kill you makes you stronger." I believe this is partly true, but if something is close to killing you or making you do horrible acts because of stress, then you have arrived where your strength has become your weakness.

Our country is plagued with depression. A leading cause of disability among Americans between 15 to 44 years of age is Major Depressive Disorder. It is easy to put on a face (smiling, it's all ok or I'm happy no matter what) in front of people but it is the inner self that cries. That dark place, so lonely that we become disconnected from within and the world around us. Whether it should be dealing with a sick family member or traffic stress, everyone's view of the world is just that - their own. We see things through our own eyes and how we process them is very different from person to person. Yes, you can generalize psychological aspects of situations but the fact remains to really understand that you have to be that person. I once got to a point where I felt as if I was becoming callous toward my surroundings and emotions. I couldn't cry anymore, and all I knew was that I had to make it from sun up to sun down. This was a very dark place, but I knew I had to keep going somehow. My eyes were always heavy as was my mind and it felt as if I was carrying 10 people on my shoulders kicking and screaming in different directions. I knew I had to be strong, but I didn't really know the true meaning of strength until I hit this point. I had been diagnosed with Lupus and prescribed medicine that had quite a long side effect list, including blindness. It was at this moment I realized I needed to seek a core inner self that could allow emotions and feelings back in, as well as health and the ability to continue to deal with life as it came at me each day. Essentially, I was blinded by the inner pain and sorrow of emotional strain. I could not see anything but a blur of the person I called "me". This was not an easy venture. I went through the death of my brother and mother in a little over a year, taking care of a bedridden father, a daughter with Reflex Sympathetic Dystrophy and Osteopenia, a disabled husband, and chronic health issues of my own at the same time. I went through all of this while working full and part-time, as well as being enrolled in college courses each semester trying to earn a degree.

I had to accept that sometimes my strength is my weakness. Sit back and think about that for a moment. Yes, oxymoron "strength=weakness" is so true. What I thought was my strength was really my weakness. It was preventing me from actually dealing with situations and allowing myself to carry on in an unemotional dark world. Masking, instead of dealing with the pain, caused constant struggles inside and out. Not a good place as I found out through much research on motivational self-help and soul searching.

What do I mean by self-help? No, I did not have a light come on and go, "Ok, I got it." That was not it at all. It was through years of trials and pure mental and physical exhaustion that I finally came to realize that I needed help. A great friend once told me she thought I was depressed; how could I handle so much without going crazy. I was very close to it without realizing it at the time, but I was able to pull myself up slowly and painfully.

Never give up! Go with your heart and gut, they are always right, or at least right for you, and you have to take care of yourself first or you cannot take care of anyone else. As my health was gradually declining, I was constantly fatigued with a multitude of ailments. I had to do something. I couldn't focus on any one task. After many doctor and specialist visits and medications that had more bad than good side effects, I decided to take my health, emotions, and self in my own hands. I had to find my inner core and build on it. I had to find ME.

I enrolled in a chronic illness group that offered a network of people dealing with situations similar to mine that offered much support and guidance. There were stress relief seminars that offered mindful meditation and humor to assist in my journey to find myself again and come to peace with life as it was.

There is a saying, "When you get to the end of your rope, tie a knot and just hang on." That is so true, sometimes you have to just separate yourself from the issues pulling you down and just be; be yourself or find yourself. Dig deep, you are in there. Like digging in sand, you dig and dig and get nowhere or so you think. It may take little bits at a time but there will come a time when you see the sand pile (realization of the stressors holding you down) get bigger and the actual depth (realization of you, your inner core) increase. It will happen! You have to stick with it and stay true to yourself. There may be setbacks or days when you get off track. As with anything worth having, you have to keep at it. Remember, sometimes like shampoo, rinse (move on to the next day) and repeat as needed. Live in the moment, do your best, and remember each day is a new day. If you don't succeed today, know you did your best and try again tomorrow.

KNOW GOD (KNOW GRACE)

It is truly amazing when you think you know God. Yes, you feel good, which results in feeling better and being nicer. Ah, yes, a great place until something comes and knocks you flat on your face - life. It hits hard at times and I struggled with this for many years trying to find myself, the true me I was meant to be, my purpose in life.

When I first set out to seek God and be a good Christian, it was scary in a few ways. First, I had a small child I was raising and wanted her to see that what I was doing was the so-called "right thing" to do. I didn't realize that I didn't really have a grasp on it myself, who I was. I was just getting through life day by day. Did I really know God?

In a search to find him, I went to church, attended study class, and even participated in events held by the church. None of this seemed to fulfill my knowledge base for finding God. No, it only made me tired with the all too busy family schedule I already had.

Then there is the witnessing, or what I thought was witnessing. You are new in Christ, or as Aunt B would describe it, "A babe in Christ," stepping out to let the world know about God. Yeah, right, the better picture here is scaring the bejeebies out of people sounding like a crazy person.

For many years, I would pray and ask for what I needed, but it didn't come, only more hardships, many of them. Through those hardships, I feel He tried to pull me back in but I didn't even know who I was or wanted to be anymore. I had to do a lot of self-reflection.

In order to do that, I found many motivational opportunities to learn where I stood with myself in life. I learned to find the positive in the negative. Some were classes, a few online blogs, and from advice shared from family and friends. What I really feel engaged me the most was when I sat and did nothing, just listening in the silence. Silence speaks multitudes if you listen. Find a place where you can sit alone, by the water, or in a secluded room. It can be any place that lets you think. It will allow negative thoughts, pain, and any emotions you have gone through be revealed. If you sit long enough or master this frequently, you will find peace. It is a kind of peace that allows you to move on or make a move in your life. Courage comes with faith, faith in God and you. Trusting that you can do and be what you were meant to be - your purpose.

As we follow our path in life, we have choices. God lets us have free will to make choices along our way. If we go down a path that was not meant to be, He will guide us, if we accept it.

That little something that is always right and when you don't pay attention to it, you will find yourself saying, "I should have listened to that little something." Well, that little something is a big something called God. He is knocking on your door and giving you guidance, and you can either accept it or not, it's your choice. I learned that it was not who I wanted to be, it was who God created me to be. There is truly an amazing peace that comes with putting God first and accepting the inner talents and unique self He has created in you. Don't let the world make you too busy to follow God. He will take you down amazing paths. Sometimes, He will let you struggle to bring you closer to his word and understanding. He also brings people and situations to your life so you will grow in faith and purpose. Take it at your own pace and accept it as you will. No pressure, but if you choose to know God, He will take you to great places in your life's journey.

Ephesians 2:10 King James Version (KJV)

"For we are his workmanship, created in Christ Jesus unto good works, which God hath before ordained that we should walk in them."

Romans 8:28 King James Version (KJV)

"And we know that all things work together for good to them that love God, to them who are the called according to his purpose."

SHARE

(Let people know you need them)

"Well, I can't read your mind..." Does this statement ring any bells? Have you said this to your children or anyone before? Yes, I have, many times. It is true and the same goes for our need for help. We cannot expect people to know what we need even when we think it seems obvious. For instance, I know someone very close to me that did not understand how hard it was for me to handle normal everyday chores when I was dealing with the many obstacles of caregiving, sickness, work, and school. He would make comments on laziness and to toughen up or be harder on my sick family members to get help. Well, it seems kind of hard to relate to this person and ask for help, doesn't it? Not everyone sees things the same as this person I am referring to had to go through some obstacles and finally realized we all handle situations differently. He never let me down no matter what he thought or said. He was always there for me as he has always offered to be.

Let people know you need them. Let people in. It doesn't have to be an invasive adventure into the hollows of your soul. People want to help, and most people who offer help are willing to go the distance for you. And if they prove otherwise, don't give up. There are some that will offer but not really want to and these are just a few.

Asking for help doesn't mean you have to bleed your troubles on anyone or become a burden if you ask for help. Sometimes, all we need is to know that people are there. It will not make you appear weak or lazy. Let them know you are tired or just overstretched in your to-do list with what life has thrown your way. Also, don't forget to pray your needs to God, He is beside you always. You are never alone and He will never leave your side.

Philippians 4:6

"Be careful for nothing; but in every thing by prayer and supplication with thanksgiving let your requests be made known unto God."

Give God praise, confess your sins, thank him for all your blessings and ask for your needs. God is good; He understands our iniquities so be easy on yourself and strive to be the best version of you each and every day.

INSPIRATION 3 – SELF

(Stay True to Yourself)

Yes, that is what I said: "Stay True to Yourself." You deserve it! There is only one you (even if you are a twin), there is, let me repeat, "Only one you." You are unique and that is not a bad thing. Some view unique as a "flake" or "standout" in our stereotypical society. Not true! Just as we all have our own

> *Maggieism*
> If you let people or things mold you, then uniqued away from who you are and who you were meant to be.
> ~Maggie Brumit

DNA and fingerprints, we are all unique (being the only one of its kind; unlike anything else).

You have the power to be what you were meant to be, but you have to accept who you are first. Doesn't sound like that makes much sense, does it? Self-acceptance is one of the hardest things in life to learn with so many outside influences reaching us daily. From marketing trying to make us fit in with all others as a whole to purchase or do what they are trying to sell to plain old peer pressure. Life is hard, plain and simple, but it doesn't have to be hard on you, the person you are. We make it that way by our perceptions, through how we perceive it to be.

Stop perceiving and start believing! Hmmm, you say "what"? Take a deep inner look at yourself. What do you like to do; yes, you as yourself, not the person that leads or follows? What truly do YOU like to do? You may come up with a totally different answer when you corner yourself within. Take time to make it about you. No, I am not saying be selfish. It will not be selfish to take this time. You have earned the time to reflect on yourself. We all need to do that more often to make sure we are on the path we were meant to be on and not someone else's path; all too often we are misguided again by marketing and peer pressure to be someone we are not. Or we just do what we have to do without nurturing the passion we have deep inside. If I can't put my heart and passion into my work, then for me it is time to move on. You have to feel good about what you are doing, be happy with where and who you are. If not, you will lose yourself in this world, instead of just being yourself. Find yourself; find your true destination in life.

Reflect on yourself; think of how children see the world. No boundaries, no stress (other than what toy to play with) and no stereotypes. Think wow, what a place to be, puddle jumping in the rain and catching fireflies. Start here; see if you can imagine yourself there. Don't think about the many tasks you have to do, pull yourself away for a bit. Let yourself go, just be you!

INSPIRATION 4 – ACCEPTANCE

(Accept things the way they are, know that they aren't perfect)

Now that you have found your unique self, accept it! I did and learned that I am not the party animal I have always wanted to be. I am actually a party nerd, and now that I have accepted myself, I am quite content with my title and have soared in so many areas since recognition. Be happy where you are. I have always wanted to go to Hawaii and other places to get "away" to a better place. In all my travels (no, not Hawaii as I haven't made it there yet), I have realized I love where I am from. There is good and bad to every place, but look around, you are blessed. Just love who you are and you can make anywhere a great place to be.

Life is not perfect! When we falter, we find our way more than when we take a stroll. This being said, having bad experiences makes us understand and learn far better than if we trick ourselves into believing there is such a thing as a perfect path that has no obstacles or hardships.

The night before my brother passed away from his short battle with cancer, I was sitting in a McDonalds drive thru. My mind was racing; just days ago, they said we had weeks and now we only have hours left with my brother. What will I say to him, have I told him I love him, have we laughed enough or have I been self-consumed and not given enough to him? All this was racing through my head as the voice beyond the menu says, "Can I take your order." I had to order for the entire family of 4 in my car. I really don't know how I did it but I did. Except the fact the drive thru person forgot one of the happy meals for my child. It seemed like an eternity trying to convince the person at the window that I did not receive the meal.... all the while, much precious time was passing, as was my brother. This person behind the menu did not know my circumstance at that time. I had to deal with this outside factor causing much grief at a time of grief! The point I am trying to make here is that, with or without a happy meal, it will be ok. You do not always have to be a happy go lucky personality. You are allowed to have your bad days, as long as you do not smolder in them and carry it into the dark place of no return. Accept the situation at hand, give yourself SPF 15 and move on.

There will be days like this, sometimes weeks. The reaction is far more important than the stress at hand. It is our reaction that causes the spiral of good or bad in any situation. If we learn to open our window of acceptance, accept what is happening (we don't have to like it) but just acknowledge it is there. You accept it and that in itself will bring a form of peace; a place where you can regroup and figure out the best way to get through it. Don't let it become a brick wall or an emotional roller coaster. Step back, be silent if you have to or take time out (SPF 15). If you accept, you can go on without any roadblock in your way. If it bothers you, consider it a construction zone, you may have to slow down a bit but you will definitely get through it.

INSPIRATION 5 – RELEASE

(Let it go)

Now you feel like you need to get rid of all of this baggage. How do you do that? You have decided to revive your inner core. You have found the rainbow of life and want to be strong within yourself and accept what comes your way. You may or may not have chosen to follow God or ask for help along the way, and you still have some clutter clouding on your way. There is no real definitive answer, but some things have helped others and I revolve around meditation. I know what you are thinking, you're thinking that you may have to go to a corner and never talk again, right? Wrong! Meditation doesn't have to mean turning into a monk. I have learned that mindful meditation can allow you the ability to refocus on what is important at any given moment or place. Too many times we concentrate on the negatives, allowing it to take over and in many ways, it will! Letting go will release the inner space back to a normal balance, allowing you to focus on what matters most to you. Acceptance is key here; accept any situation and you can handle it. This does not mean you may like the situation, you do not have to, but if you learn the power of acceptance, you will overcome stress and it will work in your favor. Make stress work for you.

Remember, consider it just like shampoo you may have to reapply and repeat steps along the way! It's trial and error for a while but persistence will pay off. Most situations are not permanent but holding onto them in such a way could permanently damage you, learn to let go.

Find your inspiration. Everyone has their inspiration. Some find it in others, what others do, a song, a movie, or what makes them feel good to create something positive in their lives. Take time for SPF 15 and find your Inspiration. Your soul depends on it, and you deserve it.

Aim high or low but just aim toward your happiness or dreams. Wherever life takes you, enjoy

> *Maggieism*
> Remember this is your space, your time, your serene moment to let go...make it what you want it to be for a release, unwind and refocus your inner self
> ~Maggie Brumit

that moment. It is a moment you cannot retrieve, a history and a part of you. Make it better or keep it the same. Believe in yourself, just as long as you accept

46

yourself and accept where you are. Whatever you choose, I hope it brings much peace to your life.

The next three inspirational steps are what have helped me to release stress. Use them if you choose, but whatever you do, find a release (one that is safe for you and others of course). Be good to yourself and let yourself enjoy life.

SKIPPING STONES

Practices I like to follow when I am in need of release or letting go of someone or something that I no longer need in my mind or life to manifest unbalance. One of them I call Skipping Stones. This can be done in several ways, literally or meditatively.

Note to Self...

It is encouraged not to throw the rock at anyone or damage anything, as this will cause further frustration

My favorite practice for letting go of unwanted baggage is heading to a river or a pond. Go somewhere peaceful and out of the mainstream. A place where you can be by yourself and refocus. Now that you have this place, you will need to find a rock. It doesn't have to be a large rock but one that you feel you can skip across that waterway and really feel the release of tension. Then think of whatever it is that is bothering you; if you have multiple things, you may need to do this exercise several times. It works best to focus on one thing at a time unless you feel it is a package deal then go for it all at once. Write it on the rock if you have a sharpie pen or just picture it on the rock. Hold the rock in your hand loosely and picture it as the issue causing the frustration, imagine releasing the issue onto the rock. Then meditate on what it has done to you to cause your frustration. As you bring out the frustration, releasing it to the rock, let yourself firmly grasp the rock to really feel the tension and frustration that the issue at hand has caused (no pun intended). Let yourself get angry at the rock, talk to it, spit on it, do whatever makes you feel good and makes you want to get rid of it to the rock. Then, when you have that all built up and focused on the rock in your hand, say this to yourself or out loud: "Today, I am letting you go. You will no longer be in my heart, mind, and soul. You will no longer control me in any way." Take a deep breath, breathing in the frustration and with your heart's content, skip that stone as far from you as you possibly can. Slowly release your breath, letting go of that hurtful piece of your life.

This practice is very therapeutic but depending on your issue or situation, you may need to visit this place often to release. Sometimes an overnight cure is not easily found, but if you stay true to refocusing and letting go through

> ### Note to Self...
>
> Skip but do so without damaging anyone or anything in the process

this meditation, it should prove to be very beneficial to your health and provide balance in your life.

MINDFUL MEDITATION

First, in your thoughts, grab ahold of the "thing" that is bothering you, something you need to get rid of or throw away. As you feel yourself tighten up inside, take a deep breath and hold it, let it consume the ball of tension from whatever it is that is bothering you. Once it is full of tension (and as long as you can hold your breath without passing out), slowly release your breath, focusing on the release of the bothersome thing leaving your mind and body as you exhale. Feel the peace it leaves. Once again, you may have to, just like shampoo, apply and repeat if necessary to really feel a release.

SHELLING IT OUT

Seashell therapy – taking your mind off the situation. And it doesn't have to necessarily be a seashell, what takes your mind off the situation can help you shell out the tension. I keep a few small seashells nearby at my desk when something that is bothering me comes to mind; I pick up the shells and roll them like dice, releasing the thought into the shells. It really helps to release the negative thought and allow you to refocus, re-center yourself and your mind.

Finding ways to release negative thoughts will bring inner peace and let you focus on positive thinking. You will achieve much more positively!

MAKE IT UP AS YOU GO

(Truth be told here, not a lie)

I am not suggesting you create a tale of your adventure or lie about anything here. Of course, tales can be fun and releasing as long as they do not hurt anyone. What I am suggesting here is to create your own affirmations. Positive thinking in the form of a note on your computer or phone to help promote self-empowerment and create a fence from all the negative we come across on a daily basis. What has worked for me is to create acronyms, abbreviated versions of my affirmations. Sometimes, our affirmations may only make sense to our inner self and the rest of the world may perceive them as a little kooky, so to avoid the dreaded kooky jar, I create acronyms.

Here are a few that may make sense to you, or they will lift the lid to the kooky jar, but they have worked for my situations over the years and continue to do so.

FOYO-SYS-VYTY

For Yourself Only-Sing Your Song-Verify Yourself to Yourself

We often times find ourselves apologizing out of habit, saying "I'm Sorry" for no reason. We feel intimidated or have a lack of words. It's ok to have a lack of words. My mother once told me, "Don't tell all you know." What I have taken from that are a few things. Don't feel like you owe the world an explanation all the time. Live, don't let people or things make you feel like you have to tell a story when approached with questions. Also, it's ok to have your expertise as just that, yours. You don't have to be a training session for the world. The advice from my mother was not explained by her but given. She let me make it what I wanted to make of it.

LLTTF

Live Life to the Fullest

I have this one on a picture frame with a picture of my husband and children on a vacation we enjoyed fully. It sits on my desk at work to remind me that life is too short to live without peace. It helps when I am having a bad day, giving positive affirmation and refocusing my thoughts to not let any negatives intrude on my peace.

GTTP

Go to that Place

Yes, find it! This means to me, go to that inner place that is peaceful. Step away from any negative or hurtful thoughts or situations. Sometimes we need to retreat to this. It may be a real place we like to go or just in our mind and heart, and it can help to readjust our thinking back to a positive place.

COWNF

Concentrate on Writing, Not Food

I haven't perfected this one just yet but I like to focus on this as much as I can. You may not write but apply whatever you like to do to your acronym. Especially if you tend to eat for comfort, it may help remind you that there are other ways to find comfort and peace.

NSP-SO

No Self Pity – Strength Only

This helps me not to wear my heart on my sleeve in places I cannot show emotion like I want to. Work is a prime example of this. Most bosses prefer to not see a tearful employee. I hope you get the idea I am trying to relate here. It is not set in stone, just roll with it, change it and make it work for you if this is something that provides POSITIVE affirmation to you and your situation. Life is not easy, that is for sure, but we can choose to accept it or drown in it. I choose to accept it and make the journey as positive as I can.

All of this, in some way, is a form of meditation. (To focus one's thoughts on: reflecting on or pondering over).

INSPIRATION 6 - BACON

Yes, I said Bacon. Now the vegetarians, animal rights, etc., please do not be offended. This is an attention getter! A lot of people love bacon (come on, admit it). About 53% of Americans love bacon! Wow, and with the recent recession, people have turned to bacon for comfort. Interesting thought, but now to my point since I have your attention.

Just like we seek bacon (or what that thing is that makes us keep coming back for more), we need to seek peace continually. Preservation of inspiration and motivation to carry on as we journey through life's winding roads. Here are a few things to remember:

LAUGH

(Don't let go of the kid inside and don't take life too seriously)

"Nothing but a Thang" as my brother would say, he had a free spirit. Laughter is healthy, it promotes happiness, and in turn, health.

Proverbs 17:22

"A joyful heart is a good medicine, but a broken spirit dries the bones."

Wow, such a cheap fix and there are so many things to laugh at, especially ourselves. If you can laugh at yourself, you are doing well. No one is perfect. Let your funny bone giggle.

LOVE

(No one is promised tomorrow, let them know)

If you love someone, let them know. Tell them as much as you can. Express your love; it doesn't have to be trips around the world. Sometimes it is the little things that capture our hearts more often. Time flies and no one is promised tomorrow. Get to know your loved ones, ask questions now. Have a get together, it doesn't have to be a planned party perfect. Invite people you love to just be with you. You will create memories and memories are what keep us going when the ones we love are gone.

PICTURES

(Say a thousand and more words)

You thought I was going to say Live in this inspiration, didn't you? Well, pictures tell a story of your life and that is living! You can never, let me repeat... you can never have too many pictures. I learned this the hard way when we lost our brother to cancer. We soon found that we enjoyed him but the pictures were few and far between. Take pictures, share pictures, print pictures and most of all, cherish life. Live it, feel it, breathe it, and remain calm in it. God is good and so is life. There will be struggles and pain but if you take it day by day and practice acceptance and stress relief, you will strive.

May you always be at peace and find time to Just Be YOU.

I would love to hear from you, send me an e-mail:

maggiebrumits@gmail.com

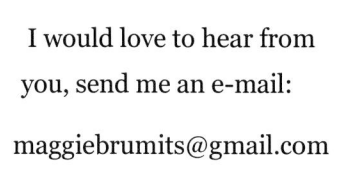

Visit my web page for more resources

ABOUT THE AUTHOR

Maggie Brumit is on a journey, aspiring to help people deal with life and not just exist in the daily grind. She has written "Life's a Beach- SPF 15 Don't Get Burned Out" to help those struggling to find peace in this chaos called Life.

Maggie has published poetry in "A Cherished Moment" by Poetry Guild 1998. Her Poem, entitled "Finally at Peace" takes the reader along an emotional path as she watches her brother suffer through the end stages of cancer. The strength he gained and the many battles he braved as he was finally left at peace through grace and passing.

May you always find peace among the chaos and be inspired to Just "Be You." Stay true to yourself and follow your purpose no matter what life brings your way.